Murphy

by Iain Gray

D1589340

Lang**Syne**

PUBLISHING

WRITING *to* REMEMBER

WRITING *to* REMEMBER

E-mail: info@lang-syne.co.uk

Distributed in the Republic of Ireland by Portfolio Group,
Kilbarrack Ind. Est. Kilbarrack, Dublin 5.
T:00353(01) 839 4918 F:00353(01) 839 5826
sales@portfoliogroup.ie
www.portfoliogroup.ie

Design by Dorothy Meikle   Printed by Ricoh Print Scotland

© Lang Syne Publishers Ltd 2014

All rights reserved. No part of this publication may be reproduced, stored
or introduced into a retrieval system, or transmitted in any form or by any
means (electronic, mechanical, photocopying, recording or otherwise) without
the prior written permission of Lang Syne Publishers Ltd.

ISBN 978-1-85217-270-1

Murphy

MOTTO:
Strong and hospitable
(and) To conquer rather than die.

CREST:
A red lion rampant holding
a wheat sheaf beneath a scroll.

NAME variations include:
Ó Murchada *(Gaelic)*
Morphy
MacMurrough
McMurrough
O'Murphy
MacMurphy
McMurphy

Chapter one:

Origins of Irish surnames

According to an old saying, there are two types of Irish – those who actually are Irish and those who wish they were.

This sentiment is only one example of the allure that the high romance and drama of the proud nation's history holds for thousands of people scattered across the world today.

It's a sad fact, however, that the vast majority of Irish surnames are found far beyond Irish shores, rather than on the Emerald Isle itself.

The population stood at around eight million souls in 1841, but today it stands at fewer than six million.

This is mainly a tragic consequence of the potato famine, also known as the Great Hunger, which devastated Ireland between 1845 and 1849.

The Irish peasantry had become almost wholly reliant for basic sustenance on the potato, first introduced from the Americas in the seventeenth century.

When the crop was hit by a blight, at least 800,000 people starved to death while an estimated two million others were forced to seek a new life far from their native shores – particularly in America, Canada, and Australia.

The effects of the potato blight continued until about 1851, by which time a firm pattern of emigration had become established.

Ireland's loss, however, was to the gain of the countrie in which the immigrants settled, contributing enormously as their descendants do today, to the well being of th nations in which their forefathers settled.

But those who were forced through dire circumstance t establish a new life in foreign parts never forgot their root or the proud heritage and traditions of the land that gav them birth.

Nor do their descendants.

It is a heritage that is inextricably bound up in th colourful variety of Irish names themselves – and the origi and history of these names forms an integral part of th vibrant drama that is the nation's history, one of bot glorious fortune and tragic misfortune.

This history is well documented, and one of the mo important and fascinating of the earliest sources are *Th Annals of the Four Masters*, compiled between 1632 an 1636 by four friars at the Franciscan Monastery in Count Donegal.

Compiled from earlier sources, and purporting to g back to the Biblical Deluge, much of the material takes i the mythological origins and history of Ireland and the Irish

This includes tales of successive waves of invaders an settlers such as the Fomorians, the Partholonians, th Nemedians, the Fir Bolgs, the Tuatha De Danann, and th Laigain.

Of particular interest are the *Milesian Genealogie*

because the majority of Irish clans today claim a descent from either Heremon, Ir, or Heber – three of the sons of Milesius, a king of what is now modern day Spain.

These sons invaded Ireland in the second millennium B.C, apparently in fulfilment of a mysterious prophecy received by their father.

This Milesian lineage is said to have ruled Ireland for nearly 3,000 years, until the island came under the sway of England's King Henry II in 1171 following what is known as the Cambro-Norman invasion.

This is an important date not only in Irish history in general, but for the effect the invasion subsequently had for Irish surnames.

'Cambro' comes from the Welsh, and 'Cambro-Norman' describes those Welsh knights of Norman origin who invaded Ireland.

But they were invaders who stayed, inter-marrying with the native Irish population and founding their own proud dynasties that bore Cambro-Norman names such as Archer, Barbour, Brannagh, Fitzgerald, Fitzgibbon, Fleming, Joyce, Plunkett, and Walsh – to name only a few.

These 'Cambro-Norman' surnames that still flourish throughout the world today form one of the three main categories in which Irish names can be placed – those of Gaelic-Irish, Cambro-Norman, and Anglo-Irish.

Previous to the Cambro-Norman invasion of the twelfth century, and throughout the earlier invasions and settlement of those wild bands of sea rovers known as the Vikings in the eighth and ninth centuries, the population of the island was relatively small, and it was normal for a person to be identified through the use of only a forename.

But as population gradually increased and there were many more people with the same forename, surnames were adopted to distinguish one person, or one community, from another.

Individuals identified themselves with their own particular tribe, or 'tuath', and this tribe – that also became known as a clann, or clan – took its name from some distinguished ancestor who had founded the clan.

The Gaelic-Irish form of the name Kelly, for example, is Ó Ceallaigh, or O'Kelly, indicating descent from an original 'Ceallaigh', with the 'O' denoting 'grandson of.' The name was later anglicised to Kelly.

The prefix 'Mac' or 'Mc', meanwhile, as with the clans of the Scottish Highlands, denotes 'son of.'

Although the Irish clans had much in common with their Scottish counterparts, one important difference lies in what are known as 'septs', or branches, of the clan.

Septs of Scottish clans were groups who often bore an entirely different name from the clan name but were under the clan's protection.

In Ireland, septs were groups that shared the same name and who could be found scattered throughout the four provinces of Ulster, Leinster, Munster, and Connacht.

The 'golden age' of the Gaelic-Irish clans, infused as their veins were with the blood of Celts, pre-dates the Viking invasions of the eighth and ninth centuries and the Norman invasion of the twelfth century, and the sacred heart of the country was the Hill of Tara, near the River Boyne, in County Meath.

Known in Gaelic as 'Teamhar na Rí', or Hill of Kings, it was the royal seat of the 'Ard Rí Éireann', or High King of Ireland, to whom the petty kings, or chieftains, from the island's provinces were ultimately subordinate.

It was on the Hill of Tara, beside a stone pillar known as the Irish 'Lia Fáil', or Stone of Destiny, that the High Kings were inaugurated and, according to legend, this stone would emit a piercing screech that could be heard all over Ireland when touched by the hand of the rightful king.

The Hill of Tara is today one of the island's main tourist attractions.

Opposition to English rule over Ireland, established in the wake of the Cambro-Norman invasion, broke out frequently and the harsh solution adopted by the powerful forces of the Crown was to forcibly evict the native Irish from their lands.

These lands were then granted to Protestant colonists, or 'planters', from Britain.

Many of these colonists, ironically, came from Scotland and were the descendants of the original 'Scotti', or 'Scots', who gave their name to Scotland after migrating there in the fifth century A.D., from the north of Ireland.

Colonisation entailed harsh penal laws being imposed on the majority of the native Irish population, stripping them practically of all of their rights.

The Crown's main bastion in Ireland was Dublin and its environs, known as the Pale, and it was the dispossessed peasantry who lived outside this Pale, desperately striving to eke out a meagre living.

It was this that gave rise to the modern-day expression of someone or something being 'beyond the pale'.

Attempts were made to stamp out all aspects of the ancient Gaelic-Irish culture, to the extent that even to bear a Gaelic-Irish name was to invite discrimination.

This is why many Gaelic-Irish names were anglicised with, for example, and noted above, Ó Ceallaigh, or O'Kelly, being anglicised to Kelly.

Succeeding centuries have seen strong revivals of Gaelic-Irish consciousness, however, and this has led to many families reverting back to the original form of their name, while the language itself is frequently found on the fluent tongues of an estimated 90,000 to 145,000 of the island's population.

Ireland's turbulent history of religious and political strife is one that lasted well into the twentieth century, a landmark century that saw the partition of the island into the twenty-six counties of the independent Republic of

Ireland, or Eire, and the six counties of Northern Ireland, or Ulster.

Dublin, originally founded by Vikings, is now a vibrant and truly cosmopolitan city while the proud city of Belfast is one of the jewels in the crown of Ulster.

It was Saint Patrick who first brought the light of Christianity to Ireland in the fifth century A.D.

Interpretations of this Christian message have varied over the centuries, often leading to bitter sectarian conflict – but the many intricately sculpted Celtic Crosses found all over the island are symbolic of a unity that crosses the sectarian divide.

It is an image that fuses the 'old gods' of the Celts with Christianity.

All the signs from the early years of this new millennium indicate that sectarian strife may soon become a thing of the past – with the Irish and their many kinsfolk across the world, be they Protestant or Catholic, finding common purpose in the rich tapestry of their shared heritage.

Chapter two:

The warrior kings

Bearers of the surname of Murphy can boast an ancient pedigree that stretches back through the mists of time to Heremon, one of the sons of the legendary King Milesius of Spain, who are said to have invaded Ireland in the second millennium B.C.

'Murphy' is the anglicised version of the Gaelic-Irish 'Ó Murchada', and the chief of the clan today is known as 'the O'Morchoe', while variations of the name include Morphy, McMurrough, O'Murphy, MacMurphy, and McMurphy.

'Murchada', or 'Murchada' is said to signify 'sea warrior', or 'sea battler', although the name is also taken to mean 'superior', or 'strong' – and this reference to strength is reflected in the clan motto of 'Strong and hospitable', while another motto is 'To conquer rather than die.'

Murphy septs were found all over the Irish provinces of Ulster, Leinster, Munster, and Connacht, with the forms 'MacMurphy' and 'McMurphy' found mainly in Ulster.

There are reckoned to be close on one million Murphys scattered across the world today, and it is the most common Irish surname in the U.S.A. and the most common name in the Republic of Ireland.

The name in Ulster is traced back to a son of the celebrated Niall of the Nine Hostages, who became Ard Rí, or High King, of Ireland in 445 A.D. and whose many daring exploits reputedly included the kidnapping of no less than the future St. Patrick from his home in Britain and taking him to Ireland.

The main province of the sept, however, was Leinster, with the barony of Ballaghkeen, in Wexford, the main seat.

This territory was known as Hy Felimy, indicating a Murphy descent from Felim, or Felimy, a son of Eannh Cinsealagh, a fourth century ruler of the province, and indeed an ancient name for the Murphy clan was 'Hy Felimy.'

The Murphy name here came from Murchadh, a king of Leinster who was grandfather to the famous, although some would describe him as infamous, Dermot MacMurrough.

This mighty warrior king of Leinster holds the dubious distinction of having opened the door to the twelfth century Cambro-Norman invasion of Ireland and its subsequent domination by the English Crown.

Love him or loath him, he is probably still the most famous Murphy.

Twelfth century Ireland was far from being a unified nation, split up as it was into territories ruled over by squabbling chieftains such as Dermot MacMurrough, who ruled as kings in their own right – and this inter-clan rivalry worked to the advantage of the invaders.

In a series of bloody conflicts one chieftain, or king, would occasionally gain the upper hand over his rivals, and by 1156 the most powerful was Muirchertach MacLochlainn, king of the O'Neills.

Rory O'Connor, king of the province of Connacht, opposed him but he increased his power and influence by allying himself with Dermot MacMurrough, king of Leinster.

MacLochlainn and MacMurrough were aware that the main key to the kingdom of Ireland was the thriving trading port of Dublin that had been established by invading Vikings, or Ostmen, in 852 A.D.

Dublin was taken by the combined forces of the Leinster and Connacht kings, but when MacLochlainn died the Dubliners rose up in revolt and overthrew the unpopular MacMurrough.

There had certainly been no love lost between MacMurrough and the Dubliners – who had not only killed his father but as an added insult buried his corpse beside that of a dead dog.

A triumphant Rory O'Connor entered Dublin and was later inaugurated as Ard Rí, but the proud Dermott MacMurrough was not one to humbly accept defeat.

He appealed for help from England's Henry II in unseating O'Connor, an act that was to radically affect the future course of Ireland's fortunes.

The English monarch agreed to help MacMurrough, but distanced himself from direct action by delegating his Norman subjects in Wales with the task.

These ambitious and battle-hardened barons and knights had first settled in Wales following the Norman Conquest of England in 1066 and, with an eye on rich booty, plunder, and lands, were only too eager to obey their sovereign's wishes and furnish MacMurrough with aid.

MacMurrough crossed the Irish Sea to Bristol, where he rallied powerful barons such as Robert Fitzstephen and Maurice Fitzgerald to his cause, along with Gilbert de Clare, Earl of Pembroke, and also known as Strongbow.

As an inducement to Strongbow, MacMurrough offered him the hand of his beautiful young daughter, Aife, in marriage, with the further sweetener to the deal that he would take over the province of Leinster on MacMurrough's death.

The mighty Norman war machine soon moved into action, and so fierce and disciplined was their onslaught on the forces of Rory O'Connor and his allies that by 1171 they had re-captured Dublin, in the name of MacMurrough, and other strategically important territories.

It was now that a nervous Henry II began to take cold feet over the venture, realising that he may have created a rival in the form of a separate Norman kingdom in Ireland.

Accordingly, he landed on the island, near Waterford, at the head of a large army in October of 1171 with the aim of curbing the power of his Cambro-Norman barons.

Protracted war between the king and his barons was averted, however, when the barons submitted to the royal will, promising homage and allegiance in return for holding the territories they had conquered in the king's name.

Henry also received the submission and homage of many of the Irish chieftains, tired as they were with internecine warfare and also perhaps realising that as long as they were rivals and not united they were no match for the powerful forces the English Crown could muster.

Dermot MacMurrough had died only a few months before Henry landed in England, and history has not been kind to him.

The Annals of the Four Masters, for example, scathingly note that he died 'without penance, without the body of Christ, without unction, as his evil deeds deserved.'

His main crimes, according to the annals, were to have 'brought over the Saxons', and to have plundered and burned many churches.

In the desecration of church property, however MacMurrough was far from alone, while it is known that Henry II had had his avaricious eyes on Ireland for some time and that an invasion was almost inevitable at some stage – with or without an invitation.

English dominion over Ireland was ratified through the Treaty of Windsor of 1175, under the terms of which Rory O'Connor, for example, was allowed to rule territory unoccupied by the Normans in the role of a vassal of the king.

Two years earlier, Pope Alexander III had given Papal

anction to Henry's dominance over Ireland, on condition that he uphold the rights of the Holy Roman Catholic Church and that chieftains such as O'Connor adhere vigorously to the oaths of fealty they had sworn to the English king.

But the land was far from unified, blighted as it was with years of warfare and smarting under many grievances.

There were actually three separate Irelands: the territories of the privileged and powerful Norman barons and their retainers, the Ireland of the disaffected Gaelic-Irish who held lands unoccupied by the Normans, and the Pale – comprised of Dublin itself and a substantial area of its environs ruled over by an English elite.

A simmering cauldron of discontent and resentment had been created – one that would boil over periodically in subsequent centuries with particularly dire consequences for the Murphys and other Irish clans.

Chapter three:

Insurrection and atrocity

**In 1641 Catholic landowners rebelled against th
English Crown's policy of settling, or 'planting' loya
Protestants on Irish land.**

This policy had started during the reign from 1491 t
1547 of Henry VIII, whose Reformation effectivel
outlawed the established Roman Catholic faith throughou
his dominions.

This settlement of loyal Protestants in Ireland continue
throughout the subsequent reigns of Elizabeth I, James
(James VI of Scotland), and Charles I.

In the insurrection that exploded in 1641, at least 2,00
Protestant settlers were massacred at the hands of Catholi
landowners and their native Irish peasantry, whil
thousands more were literally stripped of their belonging
and driven naked from their lands to seek refuge wher
they could.

Terrible as the atrocities were against the Protestan
settlers, subsequent accounts became greatly exaggerate
serving to fuel a burning desire on the part of Protestants fo
revenge against the rebels.

Tragically for Ireland, this revenge became directed no
only against the rebels, but native Irish Catholics in genera

The English Civil War intervened to prevent immediat

 action against the rebels, but following the execution of Charles I in 1649 and the consolidation of the power of England's fanatically Protestant Oliver Cromwell, the time was ripe for revenge.

The Lord Protector, as he was named, descended on Ireland at the head of a 20,000-strong army that landed at Ringford, near Dublin, in August of 1649.

The consequences of this Cromwellian conquest still resonate throughout the island today.

Cromwell had three main aims: to quash all forms of rebellion, to 'remove' all Catholic landowners who had taken part in the rebellion, and to convert the native Irish to the Protestant faith.

An early warning of the terrors that were in store for the native Catholic Irish came when the northeastern town of Drogheda was stormed and taken in September and between 2,000 and 4,000 of its inhabitants killed, including priests who were summarily put to the sword.

Sir Arthur Aston, who had refused to surrender the town, was captured and brutally clubbed to death with his wooden leg – the blood-crazed Cromwellian troopers having mistakenly believed he had stuffed it with gold pieces.

The defenders of Drogheda's St. Peter's Church, who had also refused to surrender, were burned to death as they huddled for refuge in the steeple and the church was deliberately torched.

A similar fate awaited Wexford, on the southeast coast and a main base of the Murphys.

At least 1,500 of its inhabitants were slaughtered including 200 defenceless women, despite their pathetic pleas for mercy.

Three hundred other inhabitants of the town drowned when their overladen boats sank as they desperately tried to flee to safety, while a group of Franciscan friars were massacred in their church – some as they knelt before the altar

The Wexford massacre is commemorated today in the form of a statue and plaque at the town's Bull Ring.

It was not long before Cromwell held Ireland in a grip of iron, allowing him to implement what amounted to a policy of ethnic cleansing.

His troopers were given free rein to hunt down and kill priests, while all Catholic estates, such as those of the Murphys of Leinster and a sept of Murphys in Co. Tipperary, were confiscated.

Catholic landowners in Ulster, Leinster, and Munster were grudgingly given pathetically small estates west of the river Shannon – where they were hemmed in by colonies of Cromwellian soldiers.

Swords cannot kill faith or native pride, however, and the Cromwellian conquest of Ireland only served to strengthen both.

This was to find expression in further outbreaks of rebellion in succeeding centuries, with two Murphys in particular at the forefront of one of the most famous of these bloody insurrections.

Scotland had its Jacobite Risings of 1715 and 1745 – attempts to restore the Stuart monarchy. Ireland also had its Risings, in particular the Rising of 1798 that was designed to restore Irish freedom and independence, and in both cases the Risings had the support of France.

The roots of the 1798 Rising are tangled in the thick undergrowth of Irish history, but in essence it was sparked off by a fusion of sectarian and agrarian unrest and a burning desire for political reform that had been shaped by the French revolutionary slogan of 'liberty, equality, and fraternity.'

A movement had come into existence that embraced middle-class intellectuals and the oppressed peasantry, and if this loosely bound movement could be said to have had a leader, it was Wolfe Tone, a Protestant from Kildare and leading light of a radical republican movement known as the United Irishmen.

Despite attempts by the British government to concede a degree of agrarian and political reform, it was a case of far too little and much too late, and by 1795 the United Irishmen, through Wolfe Tone, were receiving help from France – Britain's enemy.

A French invasion fleet was despatched to Ireland in December of 1796, but it was scattered by storms off Bantry Bay.

Two years later, in the summer of 1798, rebellion broke out on the island.

The first flames of revolt were fanned in Ulster, but soon died out, only to be replaced by a much more serious conflagration centred mainly in Co. Wexford.

Born in the parish of Ferns, in Wexford, in 1753, Father John Murphy was at first sight an unlikely candidate for the role of republican hero.

He studied for the priesthood in Spain, where he was ordained in 1779, before returning six years later to his native soil as parish priest of the tiny village of Boolanogue.

Initially opposed to the Rising, the heavy-handed actions of anti-Catholic militia known as yeomanry led to him embracing the cause with martial passion.

The rebellion in Wexford was sparked off by an incident in May of 1798 when two yeomen were killed by an angry mob, and Father Murphy, along with a group of other leaders that included Father Michael Murphy, who had also been born in Wexford, literally took to the hills and engaged in guerrilla warfare against the heavily armed forces of authority.

Victory was achieved at the battle of Oulart Hill followed by another victory at the battle of Three Rocks, but the peasant army was no match for the 20,000 troops or so that descended on Wexford.

Defeat followed at the battle of Vinegar Hill on 21 June

ollowed by another decisive defeat at Kilcumney Hill five days later.

Father John Murphy was hunted down and captured on 2 July and, brought before a military tribunal, sentenced to death for treason against the British Crown.

Taken to Tullow town, he was stripped naked, then flogged, hanged, decapitated and his corpse thrown into a barrel of tar and burned.

His head was then impaled on a spike.

Father Michael Murphy, meanwhile, had been killed several weeks earlier, fighting at the battle of Arklow, on 9 June.

The Rising of 1798 at last came to an exhausted conclusion, with all hope of republican victory quashed.

But Murphys would, in succeeding generations, carry the torch lit by the two brave Murphy priests, while many more were destined to achieve fame and distinction in a variety of rather more peaceful pursuits.

Chapter four:

On the world stage

Generations of Murphys have achieved international fame and distinction in a wide variety of fields, ranging from entertainment and the arts to the sports arena and the worlds of business, law, and politics.

Born in Clonquin, Co. Roscommon in 1727, **Arthur Murphy** became not only a distinguished actor on the London stage but also practised law, while his brother, James, better known as **James Murphy French**, was a noted writer and lawyer.

Patrick Murphy, born in Co. Down in 1834 had a unique claim to fame: standing at one inch over eight feet tall, he toured as 'the tallest man in Europe'.

Born in 1924, **Audie Murphy** was the highly decorated American soldier of the Second World War who later achieved fame on the silver screen, most notably playing himself in the 1955 movie *To Hell and Back*.

Brian Murphy, born on the Isle of Wight in 1933, is a popular British sitcom actor, while **Brittany Murphy**, born in Atlanta, Georgia, is a leading American singer and actress who is also the voice of Luanne Platter in the popular U.S. animated series *King of the Hill*.

Born in Douglas, Co. Cork, in 1976, **Cillian Murphy** is the Irish actor whose film roles include *28 Days*,

Batman Begins, and *The Trench*, while **Eddie Murphy**, born in 1961 in Brooklyn, New York, is the multi-award winning American actor and comedian whose many films include *Beverley Hills Cop* and *Trading Places*, while he is also the voice of the Donkey in the animated *Shrek* movies.

Erin Murphy, born in Encino, California, in 1964 is the actress probably best known for her role as the young Tabitha Stephens in the former U.S. sitcom *Bewitched*, while **Colin Murphy**, from Downpatrick, Co. Down, is a popular Northern Irish comedian.

On the catwalk, **Carolyn Murphy**, born in Fort Walton Beach, Florida, in 1973, is an American supermodel, while **Marie Louise O'Murphy**, born in 1737, took advantage of her beauty in a rather different manner, by becoming a mistress to Louis XV of France.

Ryan Murphy is a successful U.S. television creator whose credits include *Nip/Tuck*, while Liverpool-born **John Murphy** is a contemporary British film composer.

In the highly competitive world of sport, **Brian Murphy** is the name of a famous cricketer and two famous Irish hurlers.

The cricketing Brian Murphy, born in 1976, is the former Zimbabwean cricketer who played a total of eleven Test Matches for his country, while Brian Murphy, born in Cork in 1952, played both hurling and Gaelic football, and his namesake, born in 1982, at the time of writing plays corner-back in the Cork senior hurling team.

In the fast-paced game of ice hockey, **Colin Murphy**, born in 1980 in Fort McMurray, Alberta, is the Canadian left-winger who, at the time of writing, plays in the American Hockey League for the Toronto Marlies.

In the world of American Major League Baseball, **Dale Murphy**, born in 1956, in Portland, Oregon, is a former outfielder and catcher, while **John Murphy**, born in 1953, is the American swimming hero who won a gold medal in the men's 4x100m Freestyle relay and a bronze in the 100m Backstroke at the 1972 Olympics in Munich.

On the football field, **Ryan Murphy**, born in 1985, is an Australian rules footballer, and **Anthony Murphy**, born in Dublin in 1982, is an Irish professional footballer, while **Troy Murphy**, born in New Jersey in 1980, is an American professional basketball player who, at the time of writing, plays power forward for the Indiana Pacers.

Murphys have also made a significant contribution to medical science.

Francis Murphy, who was born in 1809 and later immigrated to Sydney, was a surgeon who was later knighted, while **John Murphy**, born in America of Irish parents, was the leading Chicago surgeon who invented the famous 'Murphy Button' procedure that has proved invaluable in simplifying abdominal operations.

William Murphy, born in Stoughton, Wisconsin, in 1892, was the American physician who shared the Nobel

Prize for Medicine for his work on treating a particular type of blood disorder.

Murphys have also been prominent in the religious sphere, with **Edward Murphy** an eighteenth century Archbishop of Dublin and **John Murphy**, born in 1772, a Bishop of Cork and an avid book collector.

Born in 1795 in Naven, Co. Meath, **Francis Murphy** immigrated to Australia and became Bishop of Adelaide, while the **Rev. Canon Jeremiah Murphy**, born in Cork in 1840, was a renowned traveller, prolific writer, and book collector.

John Murphy, born in 1796, and a son of the Murphy distilling family of Ireland, was also a great traveller who, while working for the Hudson Bay Company, was made an Indian Chief by Indians whom he had befriended; he later studied for the priesthood and returned to his native land.

James Murphy, born in Co. Down in 1808, was a Presbyterian minister and the distinguished author of a number of Biblical works and translations, as was the **Rev. James Murphy**, born in Cork in 1850, and who translated gospels into Gaelic-Irish.

At the time of writing **William Murphy** is Roman Catholic Bishop of Kerry, in Ireland.

The role of bards in early Irish society was vital, as they were custodians of a clan or family's heritage and traditions, and one of the most prominent of these bards was **David Murphy**, known as the blind harpist, and who was recognised as the head of what were known as the Blarney bards.

John Murphy, born about the turn of the eighteenth century, and the last of the Blarney bards, succeeded him on his death.

In contemporary times, **Tom Murphy**, born at Tuam, in Co. Galway in 1935, is the noted Irish dramatist closely connected with Dublin's internationally renowned Abbey Theatre, where he has served as a director.

Plays from his talented pen include *Famine*, *The Informer*, and *The Alice Trilogy*.

Murphys have also stamped their mark on the world of politics, particularly in America, where **Henry Cruse Murphy**, born in 1810 and the grandson of an Irish immigrant, served as Mayor of Brooklyn, New York, and also in the state senate.

Born in 1858, **Charles Francis Murphy** was a highly influential U.S. Democratic Party politician in New York, while **Frank Murphy**, a distinguished lawyer, served as U.S. Governor General of the Philippines, was appointed governor of native Michigan in 1936, and three years later appointed to the powerful post of U.S. Attorney General.

Two separate Murphys became police commissioners of New York: **Thomas Murphy** was appointed to the position in 1951, while **Michael J. Murphy** served in the post in the 1960s.

An infamous Murphy is **Jack Murphy**, better known

as **'Murph the Surf'**, born in Los Angeles in 1938. A state surfing champion in Florida, Murphy was later jailed for his part in the theft in 1964 of precious gems from the American Museum of Natural History.

Following his release he was later sentenced to life imprisonment for murder, but was paroled in 1986.

In the world of the creative arts, **John Murphy**, born in Cork in 1740, was a talented engraver, while **Denis Brownwell Murphy** fled to London after the abortive Rising of 1798, where he thrived as a miniaturist. His daughter, **Anna Brownwell James**, was a renowned art historian.

Father and son **John** and **Thomas Murphy**, from Cork, were talented nineteenth and early twentieth century sculptors respectively, while **Seamus Murphy**, born near Marlow, Co. Cork, in 1907 became professor of sculpture at the Royal Hibernian Academy.

An important figure in American landscape painting was **John Francis Murphy**, born at Oswego, New York, in 1853, and who died in 1921.

Martin Murphy, born in Co. Wexford in 1832, later became a prominent civil engineer in Canada and president of both the Nova Scotia Institute of Science and of the Canadian Society of Civil Engineers.

On the field of battle, **Michael Murphy**, born at Cahir, Co. Donegal, in 1893, was awarded the Victoria Cross – the highest award for gallantry for British and

Commonwealth forces – for his actions during the Indian Mutiny in 1858.

In the world of business, a noted Murphy was **William Murphy**, born in Bantry, Co. Cork, in 1844, the industrialist and founder of the *Irish Independent* newspaper who is infamously remembered for his part in an industrial dispute in Dublin in 1913, known as the Dublin Lockout.

The present distilling group of Irish Distillers Ltd formed through a merger in 1966, can trace some its roots back to the nineteenth century Murphy family of Cork.

Murphy's Law, meanwhile, is a famous adage reputed to have been coined in 1948 by Major Edward A. Murphy, a development engineer with the American air force.

According to Murphy's Law, whatever can go wrong, will go wrong!

Key dates in Ireland's history from the first settlers to the formation of the Irish Republic:

circa 7000 B.C.	Arrival and settlement of Stone Age people.
circa 3000 B.C.	Arrival of settlers of New Stone Age period.
circa 600 B.C.	First arrival of the Celts.
200 A.D.	Establishment of Hill of Tara, Co. Meath, as seat of the High Kings.
circa 432 A.D.	Christian mission of St. Patrick.
800-920 A.D.	Invasion and subsequent settlement of Vikings.
1002 A.D.	Brian Boru recognised as High King.
1014	Brian Boru killed at battle of Clontarf.
1169-1170	Cambro-Norman invasion of the island.
1171	Henry II claims Ireland for the English Crown.
1366	Statutes of Kilkenny ban marriage between native Irish and English.
1529-1536	England's Henry VIII embarks on religious Reformation.
1536	Earl of Kildare rebels against the Crown.
1541	Henry VIII declared King of Ireland.
1558	Accession to English throne of Elizabeth I.
1565	Battle of Affane.
1569-1573	First Desmond Rebellion.
1579-1583	Second Desmond Rebellion.
1594-1603	Nine Years War.
1606	Plantation' of Scottish and English settlers.
1607	Flight of the Earls.
1632-1636	Annals of the Four Masters compiled.
1641	Rebellion over policy of plantation and other grievances.
1649	Beginning of Cromwellian conquest.
1688	Flight into exile in France of Catholic Stuart monarch James II as Protestant Prince William of Orange invited to take throne of England along with his wife, Mary.
1689	William and Mary enthroned as joint monarchs; siege of Derry.
1690	Jacobite forces of James defeated by William at battle of the Boyne (July) and Dublin taken.

1691	Athlone taken by William; Jacobite defeats follow at Aughrim, Galway, and Limerick; conflict ends with Treaty of Limerick (October) and Irish officers allowed to leave for France.
1695	Penal laws introduced to restrict rights of Catholics; banishment of Catholic clergy.
1704	Laws introduced constricting rights of Catholics in landholding and public office.
1728	Franchise removed from Catholics.
1791	Foundation of United Irishmen republican movement.
1796	French invasion force lands in Bantry Bay.
1798	Defeat of Rising in Wexford and death of United Irishmen leaders Wolfe Tone and Lord Edward Fitzgerald.
1800	Act of Union between England and Ireland.
1803	Dublin Rising under Robert Emmet.
1829	Catholics allowed to sit in Parliament.
1845-1849	The Great Hunger: thousands starve to death as potato crop fails and thousands more emigrate.
1856	Phoenix Society founded.
1858	Irish Republican Brotherhood established.
1873	Foundation of Home Rule League.
1893	Foundation of Gaelic League.
1904	Foundation of Irish Reform Association.
1913	Dublin strikes and lockout.
1916	Easter Rising in Dublin and proclamation of an Irish Republic.
1917	Irish Parliament formed after Sinn Fein election victory.
1919-1921	War between Irish Republican Army and British Army.
1922	Irish Free State founded, while six northern counties remain part of United Kingdom as Northern Ireland, or Ulster; civil war up until 1923 between rival republican groups.
1949	Foundation of Irish Republic after all remaining constitutional links with Britain are severed.